Four Little Girls:
Birmingham 1963

By
CHRISTINA HAM

Dramatic Publishing

Woodstock, Illinois • Australia • New Zealand • South Africa

*** NOTICE ***

The amateur and stock acting rights to this work are controlled exclusively by THE DRAMATIC PUBLISHING COMPANY without whose permission in writing no performance of it may be given. Royalty must be paid every time a play is performed whether or not it is presented for profit and whether or not admission is charged. A play is performed any time it is acted before an audience. Current royalty rates, applications and restrictions may be found at our website: www.dramaticpublishing.com, or we may be contacted by mail at: DRAMATIC PUBLISHING COMPANY, 311 Washington St., Woodstock IL 60098.

IMPORTANT BILLING AND CREDIT REQUIREMENTS

All producers of the play *must* give credit to the author of the play in all programs distributed in connection with performances of the play and in all instances in which the title of the play appears for purposes of advertising, publicizing or otherwise exploiting the play and/or a production. The name of the author *must* also appear on a separate line, on which no other name appears, immediately following the title, and *must* appear in size of type not less than fifty percent (50%) the size of the title type. Biographical information on the author, if included in the playbook, may be used in all programs. *In all programs this notice must appear:*

"Produced by special arrangement with
THE DRAMATIC PUBLISHING COMPANY of Woodstock, Illinois"

In addition, all producers of the play must include the following acknowledgment on the title page of all programs distributed in connection with performances of the play and on all advertising and promotional materials:

"Originally produced by SteppingStone Theatre for Youth Development, St. Paul, Minnesota, Richard Hitchler, Artistic Director."

Four Little Girls: Birmingham 1963 was commissioned and originally produced by SteppingStone Theatre for Youth Development, St. Paul, Minnesota, Richard Hitchler, Artistic Director, February 4-27, 2011.

CAST OF CHARACTERS

Amanda Baumgart . . . . Chorus #1
Haelee Bellfield. . . . . Lynn
Kornicia Carter . . . . Fannie, Parent #2
Catie Deysach . . . . Chorus #2
Isis Fulton-Smith . . . . Flo, Parent #1
Cearah Hamilton . . . . Carole Robertson
Henry Hitchler. . . . . Chorus #3
Nicholas Jackson . . . . Chorus #6
Yazmin Lafleur-Donaby. . . . . Cynthia Wesley
Jasper Lea . . . . Chorus #7
Tanisha Morgan. . . . . Chorus #8
Tatum Morris. . . . . Karen
Tyra Ramsey . . . . Rhonda, Janie
Precia Rittman. . . . . Chorus #5
Alieyah Schauls . . . . Sarah, Patient #1
Jeremy Skoler . . . . Chorus #4, Patient #2
Essence Stiggers . . . . Denise McNair
Kendall Thompson. . . . . Connie, Patient #3
Amani Ward . . . . Addie Mae Collins

PRODUCTION STAFF

Signe Harriday . . . . Director
Patty Lacy . . . . Music Arranger / Director
Dean Holzman . . . . Set Designer
Karin Olson . . . . Lighting Designer
Barb Portinga. . . . . Costume Designer
Brooke Nelson . . . . Properties Designer
Benjamin McGinley . . . . Video & Projection Designer
Alan Pagel . . . . Technical Director / Sound Designer
Julie Odegard . . . . Stage Manager
Marques Matthias . . . . Assistant Stage Manager
Alexis Martin . . . . Student Assistant Stage Manager
Madison Lea . . . . Student Sound Board Operator

During the play, the word "nigger" is used several times. Here is a note from the playwright on its usage:

"As a playwright I feel like one of my primary responsibilities is to be a truthsayer. Whether it's writing a fictional play or something that's based on nonfictional events, at its core must be the truth.

When asked to write *Four Little Girls: Birmingham 1963*, it was important that there be an authenticity not only to the period, but to what the real individuals—Denise McNair, Carole Robertson, Cynthia Wesley and Addie Mae Collins—must've gone through. The bastardization of the word "Negro" into the word "nigger" and how it was used during this period to subjugate African-Americans (particularly in the Jim Crow South) is unfortunate. However, it was necessary for me to use this word in this play to document what life was like for these young ladies living in 1963 Birmingham, Alabama.

It is my hope that new generations that continue to hear this word that many African-Americans have lost their lives over will realize the ugliness that this word entails and its usage will dissipate over time."

* * * *

The quote that the Chorus opens the play with (pp. 12-13, and again on pp. 64-65) is credited to Angela Davis.

Four Little Girls: Birmingham 1963

CHARACTERS

Denise McNair . . . . 11 years old, African-American
Cynthia Wesley . . . . 14 years old, African-American
Carole Robertson . . . . 14 years old, African-American
Addie Mae Collins . . . . . . 14 years old, African-American
Connie . . . . 10 years old, African-American

Chorus of White Kids #1, #2, #3 and #4. . . . Multiple ages
Chorus of African-American Kids #5, #6, #7 and #8 . . . . .
Multiple ages

The Ensemble is as follows:

Fannie . . . . 13 years old, African-American
Flo. . . . . 10 years old, African-American
Karen. . . . . 14 years old, African-American
Lynn . . . . 13 years old, African-American
Janie . . . . 16 years old, African-American
Sarah . . . . 10 years old, African-American
Rhonda . . . . 11 years old, African-American
Parent #1 . . . . Any age, African-American
Parent #2 . . . . Any age, African-American
Patient #1. . . . . Any age; any gender
Patient #2. . . . . Any age; any gender
Patient #3. . . . . Any age; any gender

NOTES

The ensemble acts as a Greek chorus throughout the play. The action should be fluid and continuous.

Roles can be double and triple cast where appropriate except for the actors playing Denise, Carole, Cynthia and Addie Mae.

TIME

September 1963.

SETTING

In and around Birmingham, Alabama, and the 16th Street Baptist Church.

Four Little Girls: Birmingham 1963

(The lights come up slowly to reveal projected footage of the time period: September 1963. Martin Luther King, sit-ins, protests, Medgar Evans, water hoses, the Klu Klux Klan, arrests, etc. These images may continue to play in a loop reflecting the pattern of hatred that permeates over this "Magic City." Through these images we are unfurled into the pulse of the period. The audio of George Wallace's infamous "Segregation now, segregation tomorrow, segregation forever" may also play. A musical medley of "Wade in the Water/In That Great Getting Up Morning" plays while the ENSEMBLE files in singing these verses as they take their place behind the choir rail. This medley will continue to underscore this montage.)

CYNTHIA, CHORUS MEMBER #2, CONNIE.
    Wade in the water

CAROLE, LYNN.
    Wade in the water, children,

CYNTHIA, CHORUS MEMBER #2, CONNIE.
    Wade in the water

ENSEMBLE.
> God's a-going to trouble the water

SARAH.
> See that host all dressed in white

ENSEMBLE.
> God's a-going to trouble the water

ADDIE MAE.
> The leader looks like the Israelite

ENSEMBLE.
> God's a-going to trouble the water
>
> Hold on, hold on.
> Paul and Silas bound in jail,
> Had no money for to go to their bail.
>
> Hold on, hold on,
> Keep your eyes on the prize.
> Hold on, hold on.

CHORUS MEMBERS #5, #7, CAROLE, ADDIE MAE.
> See that band all dressed in red

ENSEMBLE.
> God's a-going to trouble the water

CHORUS MEMBER #5, #7, CAROLE, ADDIE MAE.
> The Holy Ghost a-coming on me

ENSEMBLE.
>God's a-going to trouble the water

>Hold on, hold on.
>Paul and Silas began to shout.
>The jail door opened and they walked out.

>Hold on, hold on,
>Keep your eyes on the prize.
>Hold on, hold on.
>Freedom's name is might sweet.
>Black and white are gonna meet.

>Hold on, hold on,
>Keep your eyes on the prize.
>Hold on, hold on.

>Wade in the water
>Wade in the water, children,
>Wade in the water
>God's a-going to trouble the water

>Wade in the water
>Wade in the water, children,
>Wade in the water
>God's a-going to trouble the water

CAROLE.
>Hold on.

*(This unsettling montage finally gives way to city land-
scape images of Birmingham and its streets, neighbor-
hoods, buildings, factories and people, until...*

*The projections fade away to reveal the stained glass
windows that represent 16th Street Baptist Church on
our stage. An underscore of the above medley continues
to play during this scene.*

Projection: SUNDAY - *An exterior still of 16th Street
Baptist Church.)*

CHORUS MEMBER #1. "What bothers me most /
CHORUS MEMBER #2. Is that their names /
CHORUS MEMBER #3. Have been virtually erased /
CHORUS MEMBER #5. Erased!
CHORUS MEMBER #4. They are inevitably referred to /
CHORUS MEMBER #5. As
ENSEMBLE. "the four black girls" /
CHORUS MEMBER #6. Killed in the Birmingham church
   bombing.
CHORUS MEMBER #7. I would like to remember... /
CHORUS MEMBER #8. ...the positive lives /
CHORUS MEMBER #7. They claimed for themselves /
CHORUS MEMBER #3. As teenage girls.
CHORUS MEMBER #5. Along with our memories /
CHORUS MEMBER #4. Of that horrible day /
CHORUS MEMBER #3. And what it symbolized /
CHORUS MEMBER #2. I would also like us all to con-
   sider what /

(CAROLE, CYNTHIA, ADDIE MAE and DENISE slowly emerge from the ENSEMBLE.)

CAROLE. Carole Robertson /
CYNTHIA. Cynthia Wesley /
ADDIE MAE. Addie Mae Collins /
DENISE. And Denise McNair /
ENSEMBLE. Might have become."
CHORUS MEMBER #1. Before we got /
CHORUS MEMBER #2. What it was like to have a kid's life /
CHORUS MEMBER #3. We first learned what it meant to be warriors.
CHORUS MEMBER #8. Thousands of us done already /
ENSEMBLE. Marched against segregation /
CHORUS MEMBER #5. Been arrested /
CHORUS MEMBERS #5, #8 & FANNIE. Jailed /
SARAH, KAREN, FLO, CHORUS MEMBER #2. Blasted by high-pressure fire hoses /
ADDIE MAE, CAROLE, CONNIE, LYNN. Clubbed by police officers /
CYNTHIA, DENISE, CHORUS MEMBER #1, RHONDA. And attacked by they dogs.
CHORUS MEMBER #5. Despite these things /
DENISE, CYNTHIA, CAROLE, ADDIE MAE. Each of us has had a dream.

(CYNTHIA walks forward separating herself from the ENSEMBLE.)

CYNTHIA. Seem like every day we was reminded:

(CHORUS MEMBER #1 steps forward from the EN-SEMBLE.)

CHORUS MEMBER #1. Stay on your side of the street.

(CHORUS MEMBER #2 steps forward from the EN-SEMBLE.)

CHORUS MEMBER #2. Stay in your place.
ADDIE MAE *(points to the other side)*. Meanwhile they got to /
CHORUS MEMBERS #1-4 *(high-fives among one another)*. Go where we want—do as we please.

(CAROLE steps forward from the ENSEMBLE to join CYNTHIA.)

CAROLE. Every day all we got was a heavy dose of the awful "d" word.

(CHORUS MEMBER #3 steps forward from the EN-SEMBLE as CAROLE moves back to the ENSEMBLE.)

CHORUS MEMBER #3. Don't / sit

(CHORUS MEMBER #4 steps forward from the EN-SEMBLE to join in the "don't" chorus.)

CHORUS MEMBERS #3 & #4. Don't / eat

(CHORUS MEMBER #5 steps forward from the EN-SEMBLE.)

CHORUS MEMBERS #1, #3 & #4. Don't / drink

(CHORUS MEMBER #2 steps forward from the EN-SEMBLE.)

CHORUS MEMBERS #1 & #2. Don't / think

(CHORUS MEMBER #3 steps forward from the EN-SEMBLE.)

CHORUS MEMBERS #1-3. Don't / live

(CHORUS MEMBER #4 steps forward from the EN-SEMBLE.)

CHORUS MEMBERS #1-4. Or, breathe here.

(DENISE steps forward from the ENSEMBLE to join CYNTHIA and CAROLE.)

DENISE. At home it was…

(CHORUS MEMBER #5 steps forward from the EN-SEMBLE.)

CHORUS MEMBER #5. Don't / worry

(CHORUS MEMBER #8 steps forward from the EN-SEMBLE to join CHORUS MEMBER #5.)

CHORUS MEMBERS #5 & #8. Don't hold your head / down

(CHORUS MEMBER #7 steps forward from the EN-SEMBLE to join CHORUS MEMBERS #5 and #8.)

CHORUS MEMBERS #5-8. Don't get caught up in all that "mess."

(ADDIE MAE steps forward from the ENSEMBLE to join DENISE, CYNTHIA and CAROLE.)

ADDIE MAE *(to the other girls)*. Thought "mess" was what Mama called my hair.
CYNTHIA. "Mess" means the protests.
ADDIE MAE. And my hair—sometimes.
CAROLE. The protests our families won't let us go to.
DENISE. Too young.
ADDIE MAE. Too dangerous.
CYNTHIA. Whether they like it or not we already part of the movement and there ain't nothing they can do to stop it.

(CYNTHIA, DENISE, ADDIE MAE and the ENSEMBLE resume their places behind the choir rail. CAROLE stays as the lights shift. She begins to yawn.)

CAROLE. Daddy, I'm sleepy.

(CHORUS MEMBER #5 steps forward from the EN-SEMBLE as CAROLE's father.)

CHORUS MEMBER #5. If you ain't feel up to going to church you can forget about going out anywhere else.

(CHORUS MEMBER #5 returns to the ENSEMBLE.)

CAROLE. On Sundays, 16th Street Baptist come first. So…when my alarm goes off… *(The sound of an alarm going off.)* …I get up.

(CAROLE returns to the ENSEMBLE while DENISE steps forward.)

DENISE. By the time she's getting up… *(Points to CAROLE.)* …Mama's already taking my hair out of the pin curls she put in Saturday night.

(CHORUS MEMBER #8 steps forward from the EN-SEMBLE and pulls a bobby pin from DENISE's hair.)

CHORUS MEMBER #8. Gal, I swear I think you left half them pins on your pillow.
DENISE. So, I gotta redo some of 'em and hope that by the time I leave the house—my hair'll be ready.

(DENISE returns to the ENSEMBLE while ADDIE MAE steps forward.)

ADDIE MAE. For me: a freshly starched dress and a yel-low ribbon for my hair.

(ADDIE MAE ties a ribbon into her hair and returns to the ENSEMBLE while CYNTHIA steps forward.)

CYNTHIA *(looks at her feet)*. Patent leather shoes—pol-ished—and a purse…

(O.S. throws a purse to her.)

CYNTHIA *(cont'd)*. ...to match.

(CYNTHIA steps into the ENSEMBLE. CHORUS MEMBER #1 steps forward with ribbons and a barrette.)

CHORUS MEMBER #1. Can't I wear barrettes and ribbons to Sunday service?

(CHORUS MEMBER #2 steps forward from the ENSEMBLE as the "mother.")

CHORUS MEMBER #2. Gal, you better choose one or the other.

CHORUS MEMBER #1. Guess it's ribbons today.

(CHORUS MEMBERS #1 and #2 step back into the ENSEMBLE as CHORUS MEMBER #3 steps forward showing off a dress.)

CHORUS MEMBER #3. I wear my mama's dress from when she was a little girl. The hem keep coming undone, but she swear she just gone keep fixing it 'til there ain't nothing left.

(CHORUS MEMBER #3 steps back into the ENSEMBLE as CAROLE steps forward.)

CAROLE *(holds out her hand)*. I have to remember to get Sunday's tithe from Mama after Saturday's dinner.

(CHORUS MEMBER #8 steps forward from the EN-SEMBLE to join her.)

CHORUS MEMBER #8. God always gets His ten percent.

(CHORUS MEMBER #4 steps forward from the EN-SEMBLE to join #8.)

CHORUS MEMBERS #4 & #8. Sometime we gotta give twenty percent—just to make sure we square with God.

(CHORUS MEMBERS #4 and #8 move back to the EN-SEMBLE.)

DENISE. I always sit on the front row with my parents.
ADDIE MAE. My big sister tells me…

(Spotlight on CHORUS MEMBER #5.)

CHORUS MEMBER #5. Sit up straight.

(CHORUS MEMBERS #2-4 step forward from the EN-SEMBLE.)

CHORUS MEMBERS #2-4 *(hitting one another)*. Y'all sit up!

(CHORUS MEMBERS #2-4 move back to the ENSEM-BLE.)

CAROLE. And cover my mouth when I yawn.
CYNTHIA. Make sure I share my hymnal…

(CHORUS MEMBER #4 steps forward from the EN-SEMBLE.)

CHORUS MEMBER #4. …Even when I don't want to.

(CHORUS MEMBER #4 moves back to the ENSEM-BLE. CAROLE and CYNTHIA return to the ENSEM-BLE. DENISE steps forward.)

DENISE. 'sides our skin color—things is very different on the other side of town—'specially on Sundays. Lookit how we sing "Amazing Grace."

(The ENSEMBLE splits into two parts for this brief segment. They will be known as CHORUS #1 and CHORUS #2. CHORUS #2 begins to sing "Amazing Grace" with "emotional depth.")

ADDIE MAE. Was grace…

CHORUS #2.
        …that taught my heart to fear,
        And grace my fears relieved;
        How precious did that grace appear
        The hour I first believed.

DENISE. And, on the other side of town it's—just—different.

(CHORUS #1 begins to sing "Amazing Grace"…differently.)

CHORUS MEMBER #1.
>   Through many dangers, toils and snares...

CHORUS #1.
>   ...I have already come;
>   'Tis grace hath brought me safe thus far,
>   And grace will lead me home.

(CHORUS MEMBER #4 steps forward from the EN-SEMBLE.)

CHORUS MEMBER #4. But, God's ears hear all prayers from all types just the same.

(CHORUS MEMBER #4 returns to CHORUS #2 as the ENSEMBLE finishes the song.)

ENSEMBLE.
>   The Lord has promised good to me,
>   His word my hope secures;
>   He will my shield and portion be,
>   As long as life endures.

(CHORUS MEMBER #5 steps forward from the EN-SEMBLE as the lights shift.)

CHORUS MEMBER #5. 'Morning. Wanna make sure everybody here at 16th Street to remember next Sunday's our annual Youth Day.

*(**Projections** of children enjoying themselves at youth events are shown.)*

CHORUS MEMBER #5 *(cont'd)*. Every body be sure to be here to support our youth. More information about this event and sign-up sheets for volunteers can be found in our basement assembly room. Let us observe the announcements and do our utmost to follow them.

(CHORUS MEMBER #5 moves back to the ENSEMBLE as CHORUS MEMBER #1 comes forward.)

CHORUS MEMBER #2. At next week's service we gone be passing around a sign-up sheet to gather up some folks to help address the problem of these Freedom Riders we been getting coming through Birmingham.
CHORUS MEMBER #1 *(whispering to CHORUS MEMBER #3)*. Ain't they just want the same rights we got?
CHORUS MEMBER #3. Makes you think that's okay?

(DENISE, CHORUS MEMBERS #7 and #2 step forward from the ENSEMBLE.)

DENISE. Daddy, since Youth Day's coming up can I use the camera you gi' me to take pictures at it?
CHORUS MEMBER #7. Sure can and we'll develop the pictures at my shop.
CHORUS MEMBER #2 *(taps CHORUS MEMBER 1)*. We gonna hurt some people?
CHORUS MEMBER #1. What you think?

(They look at CHORUS MEMBER #7 briefly as they all return to the ENSEMBLE.)

DENISE. Youth Day's the one day out of the year at 16th Street that's about us. All I have to do is get through the week.

(Projection: MONDAY - Image of protestors being hauled into an ambulance. The CHOIR sings, "Blessed Assurance.")

CONNIE.
> Blessed assurance, Jesus is mine!
> O what a foretaste of glory divine!
> Heir of salvation, purchase of God,
> Born of His Spirit,

ENSEMBLE.
> Washed in His blood.
>
> Blessed assurance, Jesus is mine!
> O what a foretaste of glory divine!
> Heir of salvation, purchase of God,
> Born of His Spirit, washed in His blood.
>
> This is my story, this is my song,
> Praising my Savior, all the day long;
> This is my story, this is my song,
> Praising my Savior,
> Praising my Savior,
> Praising my Savior,
> all the day long.

(The lights shift as CHORUS MEMBER #5 steps forward from the ENSEMBLE as a "schoolteacher." This

scene is underscored by the music from "Blessed Assurance.")

CHORUS MEMBER #5. Class, does anyone know what Birmingham used to be called? *(Waits.)* Birmingham used to be called the "Magic City." Do you know why? *(Waits again.)* Because we used to be known as an industrial giant, but now…we just plain ole Bombingham.

(CHORUS MEMBER #5 returns to the ENSEMBLE. DENISE looks at the black and white fountains that are on either side of the stage. She considers the white one but knows to go to the black fountain instead. She takes a sip.)

DENISE. Getting thirsty in Bombingham mean drinking at the wrong fountain can get you beat—or worse, killed. But, things ain't always horrible all the time. Some of my best times is spent hanging out at my daddy's camera store watching him work.

(CHORUS MEMBER #7 steps forward from the ENSEMBLE to join DENISE. He has a camera around his neck.)

DENISE *(cont'd)*. Guess what, Daddy? Guess…
CHORUS MEMBER #7 *(holds his hand up)*. You either come in the darkroom with me or wait 'til I'm done. You open the door—you expose the film and destroy it. Then, somebody's memories be lost forever. *(Beat.)* Is it an emergency?

DENISE. No, it can wait. *(To audience.)* But it really can't. So, I wait, watching, for the red light above his darkroom to go out... *(Time seems to travel ever so slowly as she waits.)* ...letting me know...

CHORUS MEMBER #7. The coast is clear. *(Beat.)* Now, what is it?

DENISE. I got an "A" on my math test.

CHORUS MEMBER #7 *(hugs DENISE)*. Now, that's my girl. This deserves a celebration.

(CHORUS MEMBER #7 returns to the ENSEMBLE.)

DENISE. Celebrating means going down 4th Avenue to the Pitheon Temple to get a malt or shake...

(CHORUS MEMBER #4 steps forward from the EN- SEMBLE.)

CHORUS MEMBER #4. I always get my malts at Kress's lunch counter. Don't have to worry 'bout the likes of... *(Looking at DENISE.)* Some people.

CHORUS MEMBER #3 *(shouts out)*. Chocolate or vanilla?

DENISE. Vanilla.

CHORUS MEMBER #4. Chocolate.

(DENISE and CHORUS MEMBER #4 look at each other.)

DENISE. Then, I wanna see a movie at the Carver... *Flipper* is playing, but I know...

CHORUS MEMBER #4. Afterwards, a group of my friends is gonna see *Flipper*.

(CHORUS MEMBERS #1-3 wave #4 over. CHORUS MEMBER #8 steps forward from the ENSEMBLE.)

CHORUS MEMBER #8. Only get to go to a movie if your homework's done.

(CHORUS MEMBER #8 returns to the ENSEMBLE.)

DENISE. And, if my homework ain't done then I'd have to settle for sneaking a peak at the TV to watch "What's My Line?" Need to make sure I keep my A's straight.

CHORUS MEMBER #8. Denise, what you doing around that set? I thought I told you to get your homework done?

DENISE. Okay, Mama. But, if my homework's done, can I go over to Kelly Ingram Park?

CHORUS MEMBER #8. Don't want you around no protests, water hoses, arrests. Some things a chile don't need to see.

DENISE. But, it ain't as bad as all that if other kids are going.

(CHORUS MEMBER #8 steps forward from the ENSEMBLE.)

CHORUS MEMBER #8. *Too* dangerous.

DENISE. Why can't I be like the other kids?

CHORUS MEMBER #8. 'cause you ain't like the other kids—God made you to be Denise. Swear, I think your favorite word is "why."

DENISE. She's right. But, it's also *her* favorite. *(Beat.)* Mama, when I grow up—can I be a doctor?

CHORUS MEMBER #8. Don't see why not.

(CHORUS MEMBER #1 steps forward.)

CHORUS MEMBER #1. Most times, questions in my house go unanswered. *(To CHORUS MEMBER #3.)* Papa, when I grow up can I be a firefighter?
CHORUS MEMBER #3. Gal, stop talking foolish and eat them peas on your plate.

(CHORUS MEMBERS #1 and #8 return to the ENSEMBLE. Various ENSEMBLE MEMBERS will step from their places and assume the role of DENISE's PATIENTS.)

DENISE. All girls wanna be these days is nurses and teachers, but if I can just help people… It makes me wanna be a doctor even more. And, not just any kind of doctor, but a pediatrician.

(PATIENT #1 walks toward DENISE. DENISE will shift her voice into a more formal tone to reflect the more authoritarian style of a physician.)

DENISE *(cont'd)*. How you feeling today?
PATIENT #1. My tummy hurts.
DENISE *(feels stomach)*. For how long?
PATIENT #1. Almost a week.

(Another CHORUS member steps forward to assume the role of PARENT #1.)

DENISE. As her mother, you have to make sure to bring her in immediately the next time something like this happens. You know what her history's been like with this sort of thing.

PARENT #1. Yes, Doctor.

(PATIENT #1 and PARENT #1 go back to the ENSEMBLE as PATIENT #2 steps forward and walks toward DENISE.)

DENISE. And, what's wrong with you today?

PATIENT #2. My throat's sore. I need a note to stay home from school.

DENISE. Not so fast. Let me take a look at your throat. *(She uses her tongue depressor to look at PATIENT #2's tongue.)*

PATIENT #2. Well?

DENISE. There's nothing wrong with you.

PATIENT #2. But, I feel sick.

DENISE. There's absolutely nothing wrong with you. Think you just feel like playing hooky from school.

(PATIENT #2 looks at the ground.)

DENISE *(cont'd., to audience)*. Being able to say that "there's nothing wrong with you" is the best words I can tell someone 'bout their child.

(PATIENT #2 goes back to the ENSEMBLE as PATIENT #3 steps forward with PARENT #2. DENISE and CHORUS MEMBER #8 are together.)

CHORUS MEMBER #8. Denise, you can't read all them books at one time. Better pick one.

DENISE. I wanna get this book.

CHORUS MEMBER #8 *(reads the title)*. *What It Takes to Be a Pediatrician.*

DENISE. This book has so much information. Now, I finally know what I have to do if I wanna become the best doctor ever. *(Reads.)* "Develop a strong love for children and a lot of patience in working with them." Check. "Start in high school by being an above-average student." Check. "Study hard your four years of college as you must have excellent grades for medical school." Okay… *(Flips page.)* "Prepare for four years of difficult study in medical school." 'Course it won't be totally easy. "Score high on the National Medical Board exams to qualify and get a good position in a pediatric training program." Sure… "Complete a one-year pediatric internship. Finish your course of preparation with a two-year residency. Prepare for a second round of National Medical Board exams." *(Turns another page.)* "Watching a child grow and develop and helping him become a healthy adult is highly rewarding and fulfilling work. But, responsibility for the care of babies and young children can be overwhelming." *(Shuts book.)* Guess one thing I should practice is delivering bad news to my patients. *(She looks earnestly at PARENT #2.)* I'm worried about her elevated blood levels.

PARENT #2. What does that mean?

DENISE. I don't want to guess. That's not what I get paid to do. Here's the name of a good specialist in Montgomery where they can run more tests. *(She writes something in her notebook, then tears the sheet of paper out of it and hands it to PARENT #2.)*

PARENT #2. Will they take as good of care of her as you have?

DENISE. I wouldn't send you to them if I didn't think they would.

PARENT #2 *(near tears)*. Thanks, Doctor.

DENISE. You're welcome.

PARENT #2 *(to PATIENT #3)*. What do you tell Dr. McNair?

PATIENT #3. Thanks.

DENISE *(beat)*. Make sure you get a sucker from my receptionist on the way out. *(Places her hand on PARENT #2.)* Everything will be fine.

(PATIENT #3 and PARENT #2 go back to the ENSEMBLE. CHORUS MEMBER #8 assumes the role of DENISE's mother.)

CHORUS MEMBER #8. Denise, you finish your homework?

DENISE *(back to speaking in her kid-like state)*. Yes, Mama.

CHORUS MEMBER #8. I'ma be up there to check in a second.

(DENISE removes the stethoscope from around her neck and picks up her doll.)

DENISE. 'fore I can be Dr. McNair...I got some growing up to do.

(CONNIE and RHONDA emerge from the ENSEMBLE with their dolls. Each girl will do the activity of combing the hair, dressing, or styling them during this scene. CHORUS MEMBERS #1-4 play jacks. This is a split scene on the stage that remains underscored.)

CONNIE. You hear Bobby Williams got arrested for protesting the other day?

DENISE. His parents let him protest?

RHONDA. She didn't say his parents let him protest. She say he got arrested for doing it.

CHORUS MEMBER #2. Daddy say he turned them hoses on them kids in the park.

CHORUS MEMBER #4. My uncle say it's like watching cockroaches run when the lights get turned on.

(CHORUS MEMBERS #1-4 laugh.)

DENISE. Mean, if he got arrested Bobby probably didn't get my mud pie.

RHONDA. Bet his parents got it.

CONNIE. You put a mud pie in Bobby's mailbox too?

DENISE. He the only one I would give a mud pie to. The other boys at our school ain't worth it.

RHONDA. He gonna be her husband and James Robinson gonna be mine.

CONNIE. Who do I get to marry then? You two done took the cutest guys at Center Street.

DENISE. We'll find you somebody. *(Beat.)* Know I'm sick of being told I can't go to the protests.

CHORUS MEMBER #3. Be glad when they stop protesting. Don't know what they got to complain about. Mama say they got it better here than anywhere else.

CHORUS MEMBER #4. Better than New York?

CHORUS MEMBER #3. *Especially* New York.

CHORUS MEMBER #2. Our maid is practically one of the family.

DENISE. Everybody in our school is doing something to help the Movement. Gotta be something we can do.

RHONDA. Like what?

DENISE *(thinks)*. We could do another fundraiser like the one I did for muscular dystrophy.

CONNIE. I could tapdance again in one of the plays.

RHONDA. And, I'd sing.

DENISE. I'd read some of my poetry.

(CONNIE and RHONDA go back to the ENSEMBLE and excitedly begin to tell them about the idea.)

DENISE *(to audience)*. Doing something was better than doing nothing.

(DENISE takes her notebook and begins to take the sheets of paper and hand them out to a handful of EN-SEMBLE MEMBERS who come forward. They surround DENISE. CHORUS MEMBERS #1-4 go back to the EN-SEMBLE.)

ENSEMBLE. Rehearsal.

DENISE. Remember your parts.

(CHORUS MEMBER #8 reads from the script DENISE has given her.)

CHORUS MEMBER #7 *(to audience)*. Another busy day at Kress's. Father and daughter have spent the afternoon shopping.

(CHORUS MEMBER #5/DAUGHTER and CHORUS MEMBER #6/FATHER assume their roles.)

CHORUS MEMBER #5. Daddy, I'm hungry.
CHORUS MEMBER #6. We can eat when we get home.

(CHORUS MEMBER #5 looks longingly at a small group of WHITE KIDS laughing and sipping on sodas during a hot Birmingham day.)

CHORUS MEMBER #1. Waitress, another round of Cherry Coca Colas.
CHORUS MEMBER #5. Can't we stop real quick and get something to drink here?
CHORUS MEMBER #6. Let's wait 'til we get home. Sure your mama's started to cook by now.
CHORUS MEMBER #5. Please, Daddy. Can I just get something to drink while we here? Everything looks so good.
CHORUS MEMBER #6. No. Let's go…
CHORUS MEMBER #5. All the other kids' parents let them come here.
CHORUS MEMBER #6. Only one type of parent that can let they kid come to this lunch counter.
CHORUS MEMBER #5. What's that mean?

CHORUS MEMBER #6 *(pause)*. Time to get home. It's late.

CHORUS MEMBER #5. Daddy, what you mean?

CHORUS MEMBER #6. Don't matter. Let's go.

(CHORUS MEMBER #5 looks at CHORUS MEMBER #6 near tears.)

DENISE. Pull on his shirt 'fore this next line.

(CHORUS MEMBER #5 follows DENISE's direction.)

CHORUS MEMBER #5. It matters to me.

CHORUS MEMBER #6 *(pause)*. Means they don't serve people that look like us in there.

CHORUS MEMBER #5. What's wrong with the way we look?

CHORUS MEMBER #6. Ask myself that almost every day.

CHORUS MEMBER #5. Can I come here when I get older?

CHORUS MEMBER #6. Hopefully by then things'll be different and you can come here as often as you want—regardless of your skin color. *(Beat.)* Come on. I'll buy you a malt at the Pitheon. Just don't tell your mama—be our secret.

CHORUS MEMBER #5. We always go there.

CHORUS MEMBER #6. I know, baby. But, I only spend money where I'm treated with respect.

DENISE *(to audience)*. This is a true story.

(Applause. The ENSEMBLE goes back to their places. DENISE, CONNIE and RHONDA return to the EN-SEMBLE. The ENSEMBLE begins to sing "Oh, Free-dom.")

ENSEMBLE.

> Oh freedom, oh freedom, oh freedom over me
> And before I'd be a slave I'll be buried in my grave
> And go home to my Lord and be free
> No more mourning, no more mourning, no more
>   mourning over me
> And before I'd be a slave I'll be buried in my grave
> And go home to my Lord and be free
>
> No more crying, no more crying, no more crying
>   over me
> And before I'd be a slave I'll be buried in my grave
> And go home to my Lord and be free
>
> There'll be singin', there'll be singin', there'll be
>   singin' over me
> And before I'd be a slave I'll be buried in my grave
> And go home to my Lord and be free
>
> Oh freedom, oh freedom, oh freedom over me
> And before I'd be a slave I'll be buried in my grave
> And go home to my Lord and be free
> And before I'd be a slave I'll be buried in my grave
> And go home to my Lord and be free
>
> And before I'd be a slave I'll be buried in my grave
> And go home to my Lord and be free

*(Projection: **TUESDAY** - Image of an African-American woman sitting on a bus bench that is labeled "black."*

CAROLE, FANNIE and FLO emerge from the CHOIR. CAROLE holds a clarinet case in her hands. There is a short line for the "whites only" fountain and a really long one for "blacks" that CAROLE and her friends wait patiently in. This moment is underscored.)

CHORUS MEMBER #8. Our governor, George Wallace, ran for /

CHORUS MEMBER #7. And won his office /

CHORUS MEMBER #6. On the / slogan

CHORUS MEMBER #5. Segregation / now

CHORUS MEMBER #4. Segregation / tomorrow

CHORUS MEMBER #3. Segregation forever.

CHORUS MEMBER #2. In June / 1963

CHORUS MEMBER #1. A federal court barred any state / government

CHORUS MEMBER #8. Interference with the enrollment of two black / students

CHORUS MEMBER #7. Vivian Malone

CHORUS MEMBER #6. And, James Hood

CHORUS MEMBER #5. At the University of Alabama.

CHORUS MEMBER #4. Despite this / order

CHORUS MEMBER #3. Governor Wallace appointed himself the temporary university / registrar

CHORUS MEMBER #2. And stood in the doorway of the administration / building

CHORUS MEMBER #1. To prevent students from registering.

CHORUS MEMBER #8. In / response

CHORUS MEMBER #7. President Kennedy / federalized

CHORUS MEMBER #6. The Alabama National Guard.

CHORUS MEMBER #5. One hundred guardsman escorted the / students

CHORUS MEMBER #4. To / campus

CHORUS MEMBER #3. And Guard / commander

CHORUS MEMBER #2. General Henry / Graham

CHORUS MEMBER #1. Ordered Wallace /

CHORUS MEMBER #8. To "step / aside"

CHORUS MEMBER #7. So the / students

CHORUS MEMBER #6. Could be registered.

(CAROLE steps forward from the ENSEMBLE.)

CAROLE *(to audience)*. Everybody gotta wait when it's a hot summer day in Birmingham. We wait for the sun to go down to get a break from the heat, we wait in line for water when we thirsty, but, what we really waiting for is something to change.

(CHORUS MEMBER #5 steps forward from the EN-SEMBLE.)

CHORUS MEMBER #5. Today, in history class, we are going to learn about the Republican Party and how they freed the slaves. During this time they was finally allowed to vote. But, once the Democrats took over we wasn't allowed to vote and now…here we are.

CAROLE. I love my history teacher. One day I wanna be just like her and be able to teach students that there was a time when we did have rights. But, I know across town, they being taught something completely different.

(CHORUS MEMBER #2 steps forward from the EN-SEMBLE.)

CHORUS MEMBER #2. We need to protect the Negroes from making the wrong choice when they vote, which is why we ain't gone never give them the right to do it.

(CAROLE looks over at the white kids before she returns to her friends.)

FANNIE. You learn the music for Monday's game?

CAROLE. Yeah.

FANNIE. You always get stuff done so quickly.

CAROLE. That way it leaves room for the fun stuff—like hanging out with you all.

FLO. Can't believe how long this line is.

CAROLE *(acknowledging the other line)*. They don't realize how easy they have it.

CHORUS MEMBER #1. Let's stop by Kress's and grab some burgers on the way home.

CAROLE. One day we gonna be sitting next to them / on buses…

FLO. Standing in one line with / them for water…

FANNIE. Sitting next to them in school.

CAROLE. Our grades is just as good—if not better—than theirs.

FLO. Got that right. *(Beat.)*

FANNIE. You going to that Friendship and Action meeting?

(Their line inches forward slowly.)

CAROLE. Yeah, I spoke to your mom about getting a ride to it.

(CHORUS MEMBER #1 pulls CHORUS MEMBER #3 aside.)

CHORUS MEMBER #1. My mom's talking about checking out that Friendship and Action meeting.

CHORUS MEMBER #3 *(shakes head).* Don't want no parts of that. Kids at school find out you hanging around them types you ain't gone be one of us no more.

FANNIE. Still not sure I wanna go.

FLO. I wanna go. *(Beat.)* What is it?

CAROLE. Black and white parents and they kids dealing with racism in the schools. *(Pulls book out of her bag.)* Don't know how many more times I'm gonna have to keep taping my raggedy textbook.

CHORUS MEMBER #4. How you think we get these new geometry books and they don't got none?

CHORUS MEMBER #3. Don't really care.

FANNIE. They been trying to desegregate our schools—like—forever.

CHORUS MEMBER #3. That'll be the day I sit in class next to a raggedy-head nigger.

CAROLE. This time's gonna be different.

FANNIE. Heard that one before.

(Their line moves forward…another inch.)

FLO *(jumps up and down)*. Hope they save some water for the rest of us.

CAROLE. Remember when you wanted to go hiking up to Vulcan?

FANNIE. Yeah.

CAROLE. What did you say when I asked you why you wanted to go?

FANNIE *(thinks)*. For the adventure.

CAROLE. This the same thing, right? An adventure—to be a part of history.

FANNIE. Maybe, but some adventures can get you killed.

(The line inches slowly, but CAROLE doesn't move.)

CAROLE *(to audience)*. Fannie's right, but I just don't wanna tell her yet. *(Beat.)* Let's go to my house.

FLO. Yes!

(CAROLE, FANNIE and FLO get out of the line and walk.)

CAROLE *(to audience)*. I live with my parents in Smithfield. It's walking distance from my high school—Parker. Parker's got a world-famous marching band (yep, we're that good) and I get to play clarinet. My favorite place in the entire neighborhood is our rec center. Every Saturday afternoon, me, Flo and Dianne—my older sis— take tap and ballet lessons there.

(CAROLE does a small tap-dance move.)

CAROLE *(cont'd., to audience)*. And, I've gotten pretty good.

CHORUS MEMBER #5 *(shouts out)*. Mom, tell her to stop dancing through the house! She's driving me crazy!

(FLO attempts a few tap steps of the same move CAROLE tried, although not as successfully.)

FLO *(to audience)*. I'm…getting better.

CAROLE. I'm hoping next year they'll let me do the lead in the spring recital. It's kinda all I can think about.

CHORUS MEMBER #5. Can't you talk about something else besides the recital? You're driving me crazy!

(CHORUS MEMBER #3 comes forward.)

CYNTHIA. I just started to study ballet. Yesterday, we learned what fifth position is.

CYNTHIA *(demonstrates)*. If I keep it up, eventually I'll get to do *pointe*.

CAROLE. When some of my classmates find out where I live…

CHORUS MEMBER #6. Smithfield?

CHORUS MEMBER #7. The neighborhood with the doctors, lawyers and businessmen???

CAROLE. They think I must be uppity.

FANNIE. We can't help where we live.

FLO. What's the big deal about an address anyway?

CAROLE. Most of my classmates think living here is easy…

FLO. They don't call it Dynamite Hill for nothing.

FANNIE. Living round here can get you killed.

*(The **projection** shows houses on fire.*

CHORUS MEMBER #4 steps forward.)

CHORUS MEMBER #4. Daddy and his boys gonna go over to Dynamite Hill again tonight.

(CAROLE looks at CHORUS MEMBER #4 as if they're talking to each other.)

CAROLE. Call it Dynamite Hill 'cause you all bomb the houses in my neighborhood all the time.

CHORUS MEMBER #4. 'cause you all ain't suppose to be over here. Go back to where you come from.

CAROLE *(back to audience)*. It's hard to know when your home might be next.

FLO. Sometime it feel like my nightmares might not ever end. But, then I climb in bed and sleep next to Fannie and everything start to feel okay.

(CAROLE, FANNIE and FLO arrive at CAROLE's home. An ENSEMBLE MEMBER hands CAROLE a beautiful dress made for a princess.)

FANNIE. For now we got other things to distract ourselves with.

CAROLE. Got some good news.

FANNIE. What?

CAROLE *(dramatic pause)*. My mom was invited into Jack and Jill.

FANNIE. Really?

FLO. Like the nursery rhyme?

CAROLE & FANNIE. No.

FANNIE. So that means you get to do the holiday parties…

CAROLE. Community service…

FANNIE. Field trips…

CAROLE & FANNIE. And, the cotillion. *(They both jump up and down excitedly.)*

FANNIE. I'm so jealous.

CAROLE. You should join.

FANNIE. My parents don't have that kind of money right now. Maybe later.

CAROLE. Just as long as it don't get in the way of my other activities…library assistant, Girl Scouts, marching band and science club…I can be in it.

FANNIE *(sighs)*. The cotillion.

(An ENSEMBLE MEMBER hands her a delicate evening dress.)

CAROLE *(holds up dress, addresses the audience)*. I still have a couple of years before the cotillion…to think about who my date's gonna be, to learn how to waltz, what side my hair'll be parted on. But, it ain't stopped me from dreaming about the dress.

(The ENSEMBLE MEMBER takes the dress away from her. The ENSEMBLE begins to sing "Woke Up This Morning.")

CAROLE.

    I woke up this mornin' with my mind
    My mind, it was stayed on freedom

CAROLE, FANNIE & FLO.
>I woke up this mornin' with my mind
>My mind, it was stayed on freedom
>
>I woke up this mornin' with my mind
>My mind, it was stayed on freedom

ENSEMBLE.
>Hallelu, hallelu, halleleujah
>
>Walkin' and talkin' with my mind
>My mind it was stayed on freedom
>I was walkin' and talkin' with my mind
>My mind, it was stayed on freedom
>
>I was walkin', I was talkin', talkin' with my mind
>My mind, it was stayed on freedom
>Hallelu, hallelu, hallelujah
>
>Thinkin' and movin' with my mind
>My mind, it was stayed on freedom
>Oh, thinkin' and movin' with my mind
>My mind, it was stayed on freedom
>
>Thinkin' and movin' with my mind
>My mind, it was stayed on freedom
>Hallelu, hallelu, hallelu, hallelujah
>
>Now, I woke up this mornin' with my mind
>My mind, it was stayed on freedom
>Hallelu, hallelu, hallelu, hallelu, hallelujah
>Hallelu, hallelu, hallelu, hallelu, hallelujah

(Projection: WEDNESDAY - Dog biting a young child during a protest.)

CHORUS MEMBERS #1 & #2. To pressure the government /

CHORUS MEMBER #2. To act more quickly on the civil rights agenda /

CHORUS MEMBER #3. A massive march /

CHORUS MEMBER #4. On the nation's capital /

CHORUS MEMBER #5. Was planned, scheduled, and carried out /

ENSEMBLE. On August 28th, 1963.

SARAH. According to estimates /

CHORUS MEMBER #8. Over 250,000 participated in the peaceful demonstration /

CHORUS MEMBER #1. Which culminated /

CHORUS MEMBER #2. In the speech,

ENSEMBLE. "I Have a Dream" /

CHORUS MEMBER #3, #6 & #7. Given by Reverend Martin Luther King Jr.

(CYNTHIA comes forward from the ENSEMBLE. KAREN and LYNN also join her. They sit around the record player that has a Motown-like sound coming from it that underscores the scene. The girls are having a tea party.)

CYNTHIA. Where'd you get that from?

KAREN. It's my 1954 class ring.

CYNTHIA. Can I see it?

KAREN. As long as I get to see yours.

(CYNTHIA and KAREN swap rings.)

CYNTHIA. It's beautiful.

KAREN. I like the clear stone you got on yours.

CYNTHIA. Keep it.

KAREN. You sure?

CYNTHIA. Positive.

KAREN. Thanks. *(Beat.)* Keep mine.

CYNTHIA. Don't mind if I do.

LYNN *(with high tea affect)*. Can you pass me the sugar, please?

CYNTHIA *(affect)*. Of course. *(She passes LYNN the sugar.)*

LYNN *(affect)*. And, the sandwiches.

KAREN *(passes her the sandwiches; affect)*. These are delicious cucumber sandwiches. Did you make 'em yourself?

CYNTHIA *(affect)*. Of course I'm too busy to cook these days. Our maid made them.

LYNN *(affect)*. I should've known. A good house is always due to the work of a good maid.

CYNTHIA *(affect)*. Ladies, shall we toast?

LYNN *(affect)*. To what?

KAREN *(affect)*. To better times.

LYNN *(affect)*. Gotta be something better than that.

CYNTHIA *(affect)*. How about to those poor kids who are putting their lives on the line in that park so that we can drink our tea.

LYNN *(affect)*. Hear hear.

(They clink their teacups and imitate sipping from them. KAREN quietly touches her face. CYNTHIA notices. They come out of their high-tea trance.)

CYNTHIA. What's the matter?

KAREN. Nothing.

LYNN. We know you snuck down to Kelly Ingram Park.

CYNTHIA. Have you looked at it since it happened?

KAREN. Too scared. Thought the swelling woulda gone down by now. Hoping not too many people notice.

CYNTHIA *(pause)*. My dad noticed.

KAREN. What he say?

CYNTHIA. Nothing. Mainly shook his head. Know he sees all kinds of stuff patrolling Smithfield...

LYNN. Dynamite Hill.

CYNTHIA. Yeah... Dynamite...

CHORUS MEMBER #2. My daddy and his boys going back over to Dynamite Hill tonight to "light up some niggers." I ain't suppose to know—but, I overhear him telling Mama.

LYNN. Don't your daddy ever get scared going over there?

CYNTHIA. I hear my mama praying for him every night he go out.

(Spotlight on CHORUS MEMBER #5.)

CHORUS MEMBER #5. Lord, watch over Claude as he patrols your streets. Keep him safe from harm.

CYNTHIA. And, thank the Lord every time he come back home.

CHORUS MEMBER #5. Thank you, Lord, for bringing him home safe again.

(The spotlight goes out on CHORUS MEMBER #5.)

KAREN. Do you get to hear tons of stories about the movement?

CYNTHIA. My parents don't even talk about it.

CHORUS MEMBER #7. What you wanna know 'bout such horrible things for? Go on and do your homework.

CHORUS MEMBER #5. Little girls shouldn't think of such things.

CYNTHIA. Guess they think they protecting me or something.

KAREN. It's good...them looking out for you.

CYNTHIA *(pause)*. What...did it feel like?

KAREN. You really wanna know?

LYNN. Yeah.

KAREN *(pause)*. Hoses got a way of making your skin feel like it's been ripped from the bone.

(CYNTHIA and LYNN bury their faces in their hands.)

CYNTHIA. What made you wanna take that kinda chance?

KAREN. Tired of sitting around doing nothing. A lotta kids like us at Kelly Ingram that feel the same way.

LYNN. Think you gone go back to Kelly Ingram, Karen?

KAREN. Naw. I done my part.

CYNTHIA. When my mama came home from school the other day, she said:

(CHORUS MEMBER #5 steps forward and addresses the audience.)

CHORUS MEMBER #5. I don't want y'all to leave this classroom to go to the protest, 'cause you might get hurt. However, if you decide to leave—do it when I turn around and write your homework assignment on the chalkboard.

(CHORUS MEMBER #5 turns her back to the audience as the light goes down on her.)

CYNTHIA. When she turned around—the entire class was gone.

LYNN. Wow.

CYNTHIA. 'course I couldn't get away with something like that in any of my classes at Ullman, my teachers would tell on me to my parents.

LYNN. That's the problem with having parents as teachers.

KAREN. Don't you wanna be a teacher, Cynthia?

CYNTHIA. *Professor.*

LYNN. What's the difference?

CYNTHIA. Teaching college versus anything else.

KAREN. You'd be a great math professor. You always great when it comes to helping me with my homework.

CYNTHIA. Math comes natural to me. Sometimes I think I dream in numbers. My mama told me it's a job a lotta women ain't doing.

LYNN. Where would you teach?

CYNTHIA. University of Alabama where I'd be paid over a hundred thousand dollars for my work and I'd have a long list of students who'd have to wait to get into my classes because they'd always be full. And...

KAREN & LYNN. And?

CYNTHIA. In my spare time I'd be a novelist writing under a pseudonym while I publish my math research. I'd be a tough, but fair grader—like Mrs. Perkins—and try to make sure that all my students did well in my class. And then, I'd dedicate all my books to my husband and children.

KAREN. I wanna be an astronaut. There's gotta be some woman to finally go to space and it might as well be me.

LYNN. An astronaut?

KAREN. NASA's been around almost five years now. Eventually, they gonna want a woman to do a man's job.

LYNN. While you two are in space and in the classroom I'll be a vet. I already take care of my dog, cat, hamster and rabbit. And... *(Thinks.)* In my spare time I would be an actress... *(Strikes a pose.)* Like Dorothy Dandridge.

CYNTHIA. Ooh, and you'd get to wear that same dress she wore in *Carmen Jones*.

KAREN. That dress was gorgeous.

(They sigh at this realization and are quiet for a moment.)

CYNTHIA. With our future careers we should be able to afford something like that for ourselves. *(Beat.)* Lynn, you should switch sides with Karen.

LYNN *(stands)*. Why I gotta move?

CYNTHIA. 'cause I have to practice my ushering for Youth Day this Sunday.

KAREN. Haven't you ushered before?

CYNTHIA. This'll be my first time doing it.

LYNN. I did it once—that was enough for me. It was such a big responsibility.

CYNTHIA. And, especially since this Sunday's Youth Day I wanna make sure I get it right.

KAREN. What's the big deal about being an usher anyway?

CYNTHIA. If you an usher you the first person the visitor meets. Pastor say it's like you the face of the church.

KAREN. Can't wait to show off this ring in church on Sunday.

CYNTHIA. Me too. *(Beat.)* More tea, ladies?

(CYNTHIA, KAREN and LYNN go back into the EN-SEMBLE. The ENSEMBLE begins to sing "Great Day.")

ENSEMBLE.
> Great day!
> Great day, the righteous marchin'
> Great day
> God's gwine to build up Zion's walls
>
> Chariot rode on de mountaintop
> God's gwine to build up Zion's walls
> My God spoke an' de chariot stop
> God gwine to build up Zion's walls

This is de day of jubilee
God's gwine to build up Zion's walls
De Lord has set His people free
God's gwine to build up Zion's walls

We want no cowards in our ban'
God's gwine to build up Zion's walls
We call for valiant-hearted men
God's gwine to build up Zion's walls

God's gwine to build up Zion's walls
God's gwine to build up Zion's walls
God's gwine to build up Zion's walls

*(Projection: **THURSDAY** - Photo of a young African-American girl carrying her schoolbooks, surrounded by white kids yelling at her. This moment is underscored.)*

CHORUS MEMBER #8. Last week /

CHORUS MEMBER #7. Alabama's "drum major for justice" /

CHORUS MEMBER #6. Arthur Davis Shores' /

CHORUS MEMBER #5. House was firebombed on September 4th /

CHORUS MEMBER #4. In retaliation for black parents /

CHORUS MEMBER #3. Registering their children at white schools.

CHORUS MEMBER #2. Earlier this year /

CHORUS MEMBER #1. He represented more than 3,000 demonstrators /

CHORUS MEMBER #8. Who were arrested during demonstrations /

CHORUS MEMBER #7. As part of the Birmingham Campaign in 1963 /

CHORUS MEMBER #6. Earning notoriety that sometimes put his life in danger.

CHORUS MEMBER #5. In August 1963 /

CHORUS MEMBER #4. At his home located in Dynamite Hill /

CHORUS MEMBER #3. A bomb exploded at his home /

CHORUS MEMBER #2. Collapsing the garage /

CHORUS MEMBER #1. Putting a deep hole in his driveway.

CHORUS MEMBER #8. The bomb on September 4th blew off his front door.

CHORUS MEMBER #7. Since then, his family's been plagued /

CHORUS MEMBER #6. By threatening letters and phone calls.

(ADDIE MAE comes forward from the ENSEMBLE. She removes her choir robe and is wearing a softball outfit. This scene is underscored.)

ADDIE MAE. Guess who won?

JANIE *(excited)*. Who?

ADDIE MAE. Hill Elementary—again. I threw the game-winning pitch—underhanded.

(ADDIE MAE demonstrates. Various ENSEMBLE MEMBERS take off their robes and become her six siblings. ADDIE MAE walks over to them and joins them.

The main conversation takes place between ADDIE MAE, JANIE and SARAH.)

JANIE. You was born to win, Addie Mae.

ADDIE MAE. And just 'cause I can't seem to lose I've decided I'm gonna become a baseball player for a living.

JANIE. Who's ever heard of a girl baseball player?

ADDIE MAE. There's gotta be a first for everything. Besides, I wanna be the female Jackie Robinson!

(CHORUS MEMBERS #1-4 step forward from the ENSEMBLE, playing baseball.)

CHORUS MEMBER #4. I'm gonna be just like Jackie Robinson!

CHORUS MEMBER #3 *(hitting him)*. Like Mickey… Mickey Mantle.

SARAH. Mama and Daddy ain't gonna let you be a baseball player for a living.

CHORUS MEMBER #1 *(looking at ADDIE MAE)*. Glad when I grow up I get to be whatever I wanna be.

ADDIE MAE. Baseball season's not year-round. I would just do it for part of the year, then I would be busy being an artist the rest of the time.

JANIE. Doing what?

ADDIE MAE *(shrugs)*. Painting and such.

SARAH. Painting houses?

ADDIE MAE. No…painting portraits—like the ones I do of all of you.

JANIE. That ain't gonna pay a lotta money.

ADDIE MAE. All I have to do is sell one portrait a year to live off of.

SARAH. That sounds like the best job ever.

JANIE. As Mama and Papa say, once you have to pay bills you'll get a real job.

ADDIE MAE. Least I'd be earning my own money and wouldn't have to worry about having to wear everybody's hand-me-downs, 'cause I'd have my own money to buy my own stuff and no one else would be able to wear it. *(Thinks.)* Unless they ask nicely.

SARAH. Eventually you gonna run outta competition, especially since you gonna keep playing the kids in our schools.

JANIE. If they desegregate the schools she gone be playing the white kids too.

SARAH. They been trying to do it for years, but it ain't never gonna happen.

ADDIE MAE. It's just a matter of time.

JANIE. Think it would be better just to leave things the way they are. I don't want to go to they stupid schools anyway.

ADDIE MAE. It don't mean that all of us have to go to they schools, but don't you think we should at least have a choice?

SARAH. I do.

JANIE. I think that I like things just the way they are.

ADDIE MAE. I think about the games I play in and I'm only playing a small amount of the schools that I might be competitive against. I'd at least like the chance to play…everybody.

JANIE. It would just cause less trouble if they left things alone.

ADDIE MAE. For who?

JANIE. For everybody. You too young, Addie Mae. You don't get it right now, but later on you'll understand.

ADDIE MAE. That's what you all always tell me, but some things don't seem to make sense no matter how old you are. *(Beat.)* We going out tomorrow?

JANIE. Yeah. Mama's made some more aprons and potholders for us to sell.

ADDIE MAE. How much we selling 'em for again?

(CHORUS MEMBER #1 steps forward from the ENSEMBLE and walks over to them.)

CHORUS MEMBER #1. Let me see your apron.

(ADDIE MAE hands it to CHORUS MEMBER #1.)

ADDIE MAE. We also have bibbed aprons that's going for seventy-five cents.

CHORUS MEMBER #1. What about potholders?

JANIE. Those is thirty-five cents.

CHORUS MEMBER #1. I'll take one of each.

(CHORUS MEMBER #1 goes back to the ENSEMBLE.)

ADDIE MAE. I'll meet you on the baseball field after school so we can go door to door.

JANIE. Sounds good. *(To SARAH.)* I'm gonna borrow your yellow dress for this weekend.

SARAH. I was gonna wear that.

JANIE. I'm wearing it now.

SARAH. That's not fair. What am I s'pose to wear?

JANIE. Something else.

SARAH. You always get to wear my stuff, but I never get to wear yours.

JANIE. When you get older you'll get to boss around your younger brothers or sisters.

SARAH. I would never do that. Why would I wanna be like you?

ADDIE MAE. Hey, remember what Mama says? Everything we own don't belong to us, but to the Lord.

SARAH *(trying to understand)*. So, Janie's not borrowing *my* dress, but...the Lord's?

ADDIE MAE. Something like that.

SARAH *(thinks)*. Okay. You just better take good care of the Lord's dress.

JANIE. Thanks. You always did know how to keep the peace around here.

ADDIE MAE. I hate seeing everybody fighting over something like that.

JANIE. So, who's pitching next week's game?

ADDIE MAE. Me, of course.

JANIE. You starting again?

ADDIE MAE. Yep.

(CHORUS MEMBER #4 steps forward from the EN-SEMBLE.)

CHORUS MEMBER #4. I wish they would just let me off the bench to play.

JANIE. And, you just saying something?

ADDIE MAE. I know. I'm so excited. I'm going to be working on my underhand pitch all weekend.

SARAH. Can I help?

ADDIE MAE. I'm counting on it.

CHORUS MEMBER #4 *(to audience)*. I don't care what they say—I *meant* Jackie Robinson.

JANIE. Need to make sure that Sarah gets to Sunday School on time this weekend.

ADDIE MAE. Ain't you going to Sunday School?

JANIE. I am, but I'm meeting up with my friends first and we're walking together.

ADDIE MAE *(clearly disappointed)*. Oh.

JANIE. Don't look at me like that, Addie Mae. I gotta have a life away from this family.

ADDIE MAE. What about what Mama says—that family sticks together?

JANIE. Family sticks together except for when they don't. *(Beat.)* We should go in 'fore dinner gets cold.

ADDIE MAE. What we having?

JANIE. Beans and rice.

SARAH *(sighs)*. Eck, again?

JANIE. Hush. Go inside and wash your hands.

SARAH *(to ADDIE MAE)*. Can I borrow your blue dress for Youth Day this Sunday?

ADDIE MAE. It's too big for you. *(She notices the disappointment on SARAH's face.)* But, we'll find a way to pin it for service. Then, we'll starch it and make sure it's nice and fresh for Sunday's service.

SARAH. Yeah!

(JANIE goes back to the ENSEMBLE. ADDIE MAE and SARAH are "frozen in time" on stage. The ENSEMBLE begins to sing "How I Got Over.")

ENSEMBLE.
>How I got over,
>How I got over, my Lord
>And my soul looked back and wondered
>How I got over, my Lord

>Lord, I've been 'buked and I've been scorned
>And I've been talked 'bout as sure as you're born
>And my soul looked back and wondered
>How I got over, my Lord

>Oh, Jordan's river so chilly and cold
>It will chill your body but not your soul
>And my soul looked back and wondered
>How I got over, my Lord

>And my soul looked back and wondered
>And my soul looked back and wondered
>And my soul looked back and wondered
>How I got over, my Lord.

(Projection: SUNDAY - DENISE, CAROLE and CYNTHIA come from the ENSEMBLE and join ADDIE MAE and SARAH who become "unfrozen" on the stage. A banner says "Youth Day" across it and is mounted across the banister of the sanctuary. The girls greet one another.)

CHORUS MEMBER #8. You could say they had fair warning /

CHORUS MEMBER #7. Someone called the church office /

CHORUS MEMBER #6. And on the other end of the phone said /

ENSEMBLE. "Three minutes."

CHORUS MEMBER #5. That's all they had left /

CHORUS MEMBER #4. And little did they know /

CHORUS MEMBER #3. An abrupt end /

CHORUS MEMBER #2. Inside the basement of 16th Street Baptist Church /

CHORUS MEMBER #1. Had already been planned for them.

(DENISE, CAROLE, CYNTHIA and ADDIE MAE meet up with one another excitedly.)

DENISE *(to CAROLE)*. Hey, girl.

CAROLE *(hugs her)*. Long time no see.

DENISE. A whole week. *(They laugh.)*

ADDIE MAE *(to CYNTHIA)*. I love your dress.

CYNTHIA. Thanks. *(Turns.)* Can you see my slip?

ADDIE MAE. No. Why?

CYNTHIA. My mama told me to fix it 'fore I left home. I wanted to make sure it hadn't moved.

CAROLE *(looks in her purse)*. Almost thought I forgot my gloves. *(She pulls a pair of white gloves from her purse.)* Can't usher without them.

(DENISE, CAROLE, CYNTHIA and ADDIE MAE each take compact mirrors and begin to look in them, primping.)

DENISE. Is there too much grease in my hair?

CYNTHIA. Wish my mama had parted my hair on the left side.

CAROLE. Think my curls is falling.

ADDIE MAE. My sister stole my good ribbons—again.

DENISE. What you all doing for today's service?

CYNTHIA. Ushering.

CAROLE. Singing in the choir.

ADDIE MAE. Supposed to do a reading from the Old Testament.

DENISE. My daddy's letting me borrow his camera to take pictures.

CYNTHIA. Sure my dress look okay?

CAROLE. It looks great. What about mine?

DENISE. You look perfect.

ADDIE MAE. And, me?

CYNTHIA. It's beautiful.

(CHORUS MEMBER #7 steps forward from the ENSEMBLE.)

CHORUS MEMBER #7. Y'all better get into the basement assembly room for prayer 'fore you gotta go up and participate in the service. The other kids is already in there.

(CHORUS MEMBER #7 returns to the ENSEMBLE. DENISE, CAROLE, CYNTHIA and ADDIE MAE scurry to the basement assembly room of the church.)

CAROLE. Here we go.

CYNTHIA. Heard today's sermon's called "The Love That Forgives."

(CHORUS MEMBER #1 steps forward from the EN-SEMBLE.)

CHORUS MEMBER #1. Daddy's preaching on forgiveness today.

(CHORUS MEMBER #1 moves back to the ENSEM-BLE. DENISE, CYNTHIA, CAROLE and ADDIE MAE hold their Bibles. Other members of the ENSEMBLE join them as CHORUS MEMBER #5 leads them in prayer.)

CHORUS MEMBER #5. Let's bow our heads.

(DENISE, CYNTHIA, CAROLE, ADDIE MAE and the ENSEMBLE bow their heads.)

CHORUS MEMBER #5 *(cont'd)*. Lord, we thank you for waking up this morning and letting us come together yet another day. For this is your day, Heavenly Father, and we will rejoice…

DENISE *(taps ADDIE MAE confidentially; whispering)*. Can you tie the sash on my dress?

(ADDIE MAE reaches toward DENISE's dress when the stage goes black as a muted flash of light pierces the dark stage. When the lights come up the ENSEMBLE is gone. The stained glass representation of the sanctuary is gone as well.)

SARAH *(panicked)*. ADDIE MAE?? YOU STILL HERE?? I CAN'T SEE YOU!

EPILOGUE

*(**Projection:** The destroyed 16th Street Baptist Church.*

DENISE, CAROLE, CYNTHIA and ADDIE MAE stand at different areas of the stage addressing the audience.)

DENISE. I was supposed to be a doctor...
CAROLE. A history teacher....
CYNTHIA. A mathematics professor and novelist...
ADDIE MAE. A baseball player and artist...
ENSEMBLE. A human being.
DENISE. But, in a matter of three minutes a lifetime changed.

(DENISE, CAROLE, CYNTHIA and ADDIE MAE join the ENSEMBLE as the images fade away.)

DENISE. The FBI sent agents to investigate and four suspects were identified. The Birmingham office of the FBI recommended that the four be prosecuted.
CYNTHIA. However, the director of the FBI, J. Edgar Hoover, refused and claimed that civil rights activists themselves bombed the church to gain public sympathy. The FBI initially closed the case in 1968.
CAROLE. The suspects were four members of the Ku Klux Klan. It took nearly forty years for them to be brought to justice. Local prosecutors reopened the case and one suspect, Robert "Dynamite Bob" Chambliss, was convicted of murder in 1977.
ADDIE MAE. Herman Cash died in 1994 as charges against him were being prepared. On May 1, 2001, a

Birmingham jury convicted Thomas Blanton (sixty-two years old at the time of the trial) on four counts of murder. Finally, on May 22, 2002, a jury convicted Bobby Frank Cherry of the murders. Both Blanton and Cherry were sentenced to life in prison.

(The underscore of the song "Lift Every Voice and Sing" plays underneath the ENSEMBLE.)

CHORUS MEMBER #1. "What bothers me most /
CHORUS MEMBER #2. Is that their names /
CHORUS MEMBER #3. Have been virtually erased /
CHORUS MEMBER #5. Erased!
CHORUS MEMBER #4. They are inevitably referred to /
CHORUS MEMBER #5. As
ENSEMBLE. "the four black girls" /
CHORUS MEMBER #6. Killed in the Birmingham church bombing.
CHORUS MEMBER #7. I would like to remember… /
CHORUS MEMBER #8. …the positive lives /
CHORUS MEMBER #7. They claimed for themselves /
CHORUS MEMBER #3. As teenage girls.
CHORUS MEMBER #5. Along with our memories /
CHORUS MEMBER #4. Of that horrible day /
CHORUS MEMBER #3. And what it symbolized /
CHORUS MEMBER #2. I would also like us all to consider what /

(CAROLE, CYNTHIA, ADDIE MAE and DENISE slowly emerge from the ENSEMBLE as each of them state their names.)

LYNN.
>Lift every voice and sing,
>Till earth and heaven ring,

CAROLE. Carole Robertson /
CHORUS MEMBER #8. Ring with the harmonies of liberty;
CYNTHIA. Cynthia Wesley /
SARAH. Let our rejoicing rise
ADDIE MAE. Addie Mae Collins /
CHORUS MEMBER #3. High as the listening skies,
DENISE. And Denise McNair /
LYNN, CHORUS MEMBER #8, SARAH, CHORUS MEMBER #3. Let it resound loud as the rolling sea.
ENSEMBLE. Might have become."

(The ENSEMBLE begins to sing "Lift Every Voice and Sing."

*The **projections** begin to show images of prominent African-Americans who have existed throughout recent history to the present.)*

ENSEMBLE *(cont'd)*.
>Sing a song full of the faith that the
>Dark past has taught us,
>Sing a song full of the hope that the present has
>>brought us;
>Facing the rising sun of our new day begun,
>Let us march on till victory is won.

Stony the road we trod,
Bitter the chastening rod,
Felt in the days when hope unborn had died;
Yet with a steady beat,
Have not our weary feet
Come to the place
For which our fathers died?

We have come over a way that with tears have been
    watered,
We have come, treading our path through the blood
    of the slaughtered,
Out from the gloomy past,
Till now we stand at last
Where the white gleam
Of our bright star is cast.

JANIE.

God of our weary years,
God of our silent tears,

Thou who hast brought us thus far on the way;
Thou who hast by thy might led us into the light,
Keep us forever in the path, we pray.

ENSEMBLE.

Lest our feet stray from the places, our God, where
    we met thee;
Lest our hearts drunk with the wine of the world, we
    forget thee,

(DENISE, CYNTHIA, CAROLE and ADDIE MAE move away from the ENSEMBLE holding little chalkboards.)

CAROLE, DENISE, CYNTHIA, ADDIE MAE.
    Shadowed beneath thy hand,
    May we forever stand,

ENSEMBLE.
    True to our God,
    True to our native land.

    True to our God,
    True to our native land.

    True to our God,
    True to our native land.

(As each of them flip the chalkboards over it asks the question: "Who Will You Be?"

Lights fade.)

END OF PLAY

NOTES

NOTES

NOTES

NOTES

NOTES